A HEALING WORD

A HEALING WORD

A Reflective Journey Towards Inner Peace

John A. Flanagan

VERITAS

First published 2009 by
Veritas Publications
7–8 Lower Abbey Street
Dublin 1
Ireland
Email publications@veritas.ie
Website www.veritas.ie

ISBN 978 1 84730 160 4

Reprinted 2009, 2012

10 9 8 7 6 5 4 3

Scripture taken from The Jerusalem Bible © 1966, 1967 and 1968 by
Darton, Longman & Todd Ltd and Doubleday & Company, Inc., except
for Scripture in 'Restoring Your Good Name', which is taken from The
New Jerusalem Bible © 1985 by Darton, Longman & Todd Ltd and
Doubleday & Company Inc.

A catalogue record for this book is available from the British Library.

Designed by Niamh McGarry

Printed in the Republic of Ireland by Gemini International, Dublin

*Veritas books are printed on paper made from the wood pulp of managed
forests. For every tree felled, at least one tree is planted, thereby renewing
natural resources.*

In Loving Memory of My Parents

'Your love is everlasting.'
Psalm 138:8

ACKNOWLEDGEMENTS

My special thanks to my family and to my friends for their constant love and care and for their support in writing this book.

My special thanks also to the people I serve in my ministry for their sharing of faith and their kindness.

CONTENTS

INVISIBLE

SCRIPTURE

There was a woman who had suffered from a haemorrhage for twelve years; after long and painful treatment under various doctors, she had spent all she had without being any the better for it, in fact, she was getting worse. She had heard about Jesus, and she came up behind him through the crowd and touched his cloak. 'If I can touch even his clothes,' she had told herself, 'I shall be well again.' And the source of her bleeding dried up instantly, and she felt in herself that she was cured of her complaint. Immediately aware that power had gone out from him, Jesus turned round in the crowd and said, 'Who touched my clothes?' His disciples said to him, 'You see how the crowd is round you and yet you say, "Who touched me?"' But he continued to look all around to see who had done it. Then the woman came forward, frightened and trembling because she knew what had happened to her, and she fell at his feet and told him the whole truth. 'My daughter,' he said 'your faith has restored you to health; go in peace and be free from your complaint.'

Mark 5:25-34

IDENTIFYING OBSTACLES

- Do I appreciate the people in my life that watch over and care about me?

- Am I aware of God's loving presence in me through the Holy Spirit?

- When I face difficult problems in my life, do I reach out to Jesus with the same conviction as the woman who suffered for twelve years?

- Am I a source of strength to others?

REFLECTION

Many public buildings are fitted with surveillance equipment that is invisible to the naked eye, yet this equipment is responsive when necessary. It makes the buildings' doors respond to us, directing us to enter and exit without effort.

There are other types of invisible surveillance in our lives which direct us: those whose inner sense of what we need watch over us and open the right doors for us where possible. We experience this inner sense in those who care and love us: parents, teachers, pastors, mentors and workers in our communities who organise life-enriching activities for us. God's invisible but real presence is there in so many people helping to open doors for us.

The woman with the haemorrhage is dealing with a physical complaint, but she is also dealing with a spiritual one: she is searching for the right way forward. The odds seem stacked against her. For example, medicine failed her; society ignored her; her sickness isolated her; she was broken on every level. Nobody cared enough about her to bring her to Jesus. The crowd pressing around Jesus ignored her, yet she believed that if she could touch his clothes, she would be well again. Jesus opens the door to physical healing for her as a way of opening the door to hope. He shows her that the care of God is as real as that healing, even though it is not always visible.

Jesus opens the way to faith for the woman and we can learn from her experience. God's power prevails in us when we put our faith in him. He will also help us to find a way through problems and difficulties, where otherwise doubt and despair might fester in us. Jesus opens the way to faith for the woman so that the work of the Holy Spirit will bear fruit in us, so that we too will believe that God is keeping the right doors in life primed to open for us.

There is much in life that works against such faith: bad things, accidents and illness, problems that appear insurmountable. The story of the woman is for our benefit, so that we will not lose trust in the God who loves us and watches over us in ways that we are not always aware of.

A Personal Response

- Ask a friend or someone you know and respect to help you find a way through the difficulty you might be in.

- Support someone you know who is suffering at present or who is finding life problematic.

- Perhaps you might read the Scripture passage again while asking God to help you have faith that he is keeping the right doors open to you in your life.

A Prayer for the Journey

Loving Lord,

You are always near.
Your Spirit is in me watching over me, even though I am not always aware of it.
Help me to put my faith wholeheartedly in you when I find the journey tough. Increase my faith and restore my hope in you so that I am always aware that you are with me and that, in the support of others, you are helping doors to open for me through difficult situations.

I pray through Jesus Christ, Our Lord. Amen.

LIFE-CHANGING MOMENTS

Jesus took with him Peter and James and his brother John and led them up a high mountain where they could be alone. There in their presence he was transfigured: his face shone like the sun and his clothes became as white as the light. Suddenly Moses and Elijah appeared to them; they were talking with him. Then Peter spoke to Jesus. 'Lord,' he said, 'it is wonderful for us to be here; if you wish, I will make three tents here, one for you, one for Moses and one for Elijah.' He was still speaking when suddenly a bright cloud covered them with shadow, and from the cloud there came a voice which said, 'This is my Son, the Beloved; he enjoys my favour. Listen to him'. When they heard this, the disciples fell on their faces, overcome with fear. But Jesus came up and touched them. 'Stand up,' he said, 'do not be afraid.' And when they raised their eyes they saw no one but only Jesus.

Matthew 17:1-8

IDENTIFYING OBSTACLES

- Do I take time to notice the beauty and glory of God breaking through in the world of nature?

- Do I allow my spirit to rejoice in the splendour of God's Creation?

- Is my mind too cluttered with the worries and concerns of everyday to notice the sights and sounds around me that are real?

REFLECTION

Maybe you have been in a lovely place where you felt a beautiful sense of unity with God in his Creation. You may have gone for a walk and basked in the serenity of a quiet sunset beach where the waning sun rested between heaven and earth after its day's work. Perhaps the warm sea dappled red rays in front of you as if honouring your presence, while the tide splashed gently, caressing your feet. On another occasion you may have taken a walk across the hills in the local countryside on a summer's day. Here you observed the beauty of God's creation as breathtaking and transfiguring: sweeping landscapes rubbing against the sky, parked trees nodding as you pass by, flowers faithfully colouring the way in front of you.

Such glorious moments with God in the sanctuary of Creation offers the space to renew your energy and zest for life. It is an opportunity to reflect on and rediscover your identity in the world as a child of God – you are loved by God and God only wants the best for you. These quiet moments bring calmness and a fresh sense of focus, which promotes a greater sense of harmony in life. These moments can be called transfiguration moments, because your energy is renewed and you are offered support to move forward in faith to the joy and glory that awaits you in heaven.

Jesus led three apostles up a mountain to give them a glimpse of the glory that lay ahead, which Jesus knew would stand them in good stead when he would no longer be with them. Jesus tells them to 'stand up' and 'do not be afraid' and not to '[fall] on their faces' when challenges, fear and doubt confront them. The identity of Jesus is made very clear to them when God says, 'This is my Son, the Beloved; he enjoys my favour. Listen to him'.

Our experience may not be as life-changing as that of the apostles; nevertheless, it strengthens our endurance to continue on our path to the glory that awaits us in heaven. We need to allow ourselves some well-deserved quality time and space to declutter our minds and hearts so that we will feel God's gentle presence and breathe afresh God's encouraging advice to 'stand up' and 'not be afraid' as we follow Jesus on our journey to heaven. Before Jesus entered into the full glory of heaven with God the Father, he underwent the excruciating pain of the cross. Even Jesus was not exempt from suffering. His transfiguration on the mountain gives us a purpose and a reason to 'stand up' and 'not be afraid' as we journey to the glory of heaven.

A Personal Response

- Go for an invigorating walk in the countryside, looking and listening to the sounds of nature.

- Take time to reflect and to see the image of God in the scenery around you.

- Listen to God speaking softly to you in the calmness and tranquility within your heart.

- Allow this walk to be a small life-changing moment to give you hope and perseverence as you reflect on the glory of heaven that awaits you.

A Prayer for the Journey

Loving Lord,

You care for me so much that you revealed on the mountain the glory that awaits me.

Before you entered into the full glory of heaven, you suffered first. I know that suffering is part of the journey, but fill me with your courage to never give up and to keep focusing on the glory that awaits me in heaven.

May I always find space and time in my life to listen to your reinvigorating words to 'stand up' and 'not be afraid'. Help me not to lose sight of heaven.

May others see a glimpse of your glory shining through me in who I am and how I live.

I pray through Jesus Christ, Our Lord. Amen.

WELCOME HOME

> I will leave this place and go to my father and say: 'Father, I have sinned against heaven and against you; I no longer deserve to be called your son; treat me as one of your paid servants.' So he left the place and went back to his father. While he was still a long way off, his father saw him and was moved with pity. He ran to the boy, clasped him in his arms and kissed him tenderly ... The father said to his servants, 'Quick! Bring the calf we have been fattening, and kill it; we are going to have a feast, a celebration, because this son of mine was dead and has come back to life; he was lost and is found'.
>
> *Luke 15:18-20, 22-24*

IDENTIFYING OBSTACLES

- What have I done to distance myself from God?

- Is there something I find difficult to say sorry to God for?

- Do I need to be reconciled with God? How do I begin the process?

REFLECTION

Life experiences colour our faith and affect our capacity for God. We may not see God as a God we can return to. If we have made mistakes like the Prodigal Son, we may find it difficult to come and say sorry to God. This may be due to our inherited understanding of God.

Nobody gets to make a brand new start, but everyone can make a new ending. We cannot change what has happened to us, nor can we change what we have done wrong. To help us to make a new ending to our lives, Jesus gives us an image of God that is all-loving – after all, he is talking about his Father in heaven. We are given an image of God as one who loves us, worries about us, cares about us and who is always waiting for us to return to him at any time. He rejoices when we do so. Every day the son's father gazed wistfully into the distance in the hope that he might see his son returning home.

Interestingly, it is not known how long the son stayed away; it may have been six months or six years. Obviously this was not an important detail for Jesus. What was important was that when the son eventually returned, he received a welcome beyond his imagination. His father 'was moved with pity. He ran to the boy and clasped him in his arms and kissed him tenderly'. He told his servants to organise a feast to celebrate his son's return, because 'this son of mine was dead and has come back to life; he was lost and is found'. The father's loving actions displayed his deep love for his son and proved how precious his son was to him.

The image Jesus gives us of God is central to his teaching. In this parable Jesus is emphasising how precious we are to God. We are his children, we belong to him. He emphasises that God is like a loving parent who loves a son or daughter no matter what they have done. The father in the parable never stopped loving his son, which explains why he reacted in such an excited and loving manner when he saw his son coming from a distance. Jesus tells us that we are always in God's love. God loves us even more than we love ourselves. There is never a moment that God stops loving us.

The son would not have fully appreciated the depth of his father's love for him if he had decided to stay away. Jesus tells this parable of a father's love for his son to show us that it is never too late to respond to God's love. Whatever image of God we may have inherited, Jesus gives us the most wonderful image of God as a parent that never stops loving us, and who is always waiting patiently and lovingly for us to return to him.

A Personal Response

- Recall an occasion when you acted very selfishly. Who was affected by your actions? Offer an apology if it is not too late.

- Think of someone to whom you need to say sorry. Reflect for a moment as to how you might do this. What lessons might you learn from Jesus?

- Tell God you are sorry for a sin you committed that distanced you from him for a long period of time, so that you can enjoy God's healing love for you. Celebrate this wonderful moment in some way.

A Prayer for the Journey

Loving Lord,
I am always in your love.
You never stop loving me even when I stray away from you.
Even when I sin, you wait patiently for me to return to you and to welcome me back with open arms. Through your Spirit, redirect me so that I can come into the fullness of your healing love. In the same way you forgive me, increase your grace in me so that I may be reconciled with those I may have hurt or those who have hurt me.

I pray through Jesus Christ, Our Lord. Amen.

WHAT IS ON OFFER FROM JESUS?

SCRIPTURE

> Martha said to Jesus, 'If you had been here, my
> brother would not have died, but I know that, even
> now, whatever you ask of God, he will grant you'.
> 'Your brother,' said Jesus to her, 'will rise again.'
> Martha said, 'I know he will rise again at the
> resurrection on the last day'. Jesus said: 'I am the
> resurrection. If anyone believes in me, even though
> he dies he will live, and whoever lives and belives in
> me will never die. Do you believe this?' 'Yes, Lord,'
> she said, 'I believe that you are the Christ, the Son
> of God, the one who was to come into this world.'
> *John 11:21-27*

IDENTIFYING OBSTACLES

- Do I accept what Jesus is offering me?

- Am I influenced too much by the promises of this
  world so that I overlook what Jesus is offering?

- Do I bring hope to others?

Reflection

Even though the land in winter appears dull and lifeless, spring brings a new season with a new colour and a new look. Witnessing the birth of new life from the earth's womb uplifts the human spirit. During the beautiful season of spring, nature unfolds a symphony of sight, sound and sense: the birds, the flowers, the trees and the blades of grass become a prayer of praise. Nature is a great witness.

We celebrate resurrection moments in life: the sweet taste of success in sports, in studies or in relationships, which is often preceded by work and sacrifice. There was a story about the anguish a young married man experienced when he was made redundant, despite the years of dedication to his job. When his children came home from school one evening, his eight-year-old daughter innocently said: 'Daddy, I'm glad you are not working because you are always here to hug me when I come home from school.' Suddenly it dawned on him that his job had consumed him too much, to the detriment of his family. Thankfully for him he found new employment, but claimed that he had learned a valuable lesson. His daughter's innocent words changed his attitude towards work.

For him it was not a resurrection in the complete sense of the word, but in a very real sense he was awakened to new life. Jesus affirms this pattern of new life following loss. The young married man realised that life goes on, along with the new experiences that come with it – in his case the appreciation for the love and joy of his family. Ironically, the loss of his job transformed his view and outlook in life. For him his loss was life-changing.

Jesus offers us a new life through him. He offers us a new way of seeing things, a fresh perspective on life. Through Jesus we know that new life will follow this life. Jesus helps us to see new reasons for getting up and trying again. Jesus invites us to be open to a new existence always, and through what Jesus did we find meaning to the losses we experience in our lives. Jesus said: 'I am the resurrection. Nobody can come to the Father except through me.' Jesus' death was not the end but the beginning of a new life for him in heaven and the revelation of a new life for us in heaven.

When the landscape of our lives appears dark, Jesus would want his words, 'I am the resurrection' to be a light from beyond our present happenings towards a new life.

A Personal Response

- Reflect on an experience that made you think more about the meaning of life. What was it? Who guided you through it?

- Spend some time reflecting on how the experience of Jesus in his death and resurrection reveals that new life is always positive. Slowly allow this hope of new life to help you cope more positively with any losses or disappointments in your life.

- Heighten your sensitivity and empathy to the needs of others in your community. Think how they too need the promises of a new life beyond life's difficult moments.

- Explore how you might help someone to live into new hope.

A Prayer for the Journey

Loving Lord,

Thank you for promising me the gift of a life in heaven where all is made new, where all is restored.
I am grateful and humbled to be offered such a glorious gift.
You offer me new reasons to find meaning and to continue on my journey, even in my times of loss and disappointment. May your promise bring healing and inner peace and renewed energy on my journey to heaven. Help me to be a source of new life to others by the way I live my life and through supporting others in times of difficulty.

I pray through Jesus Christ, Our Lord. Amen.

THE LASTING LEGACY OF BAPTISM

Hope is not deceptive, because the love of God has been poured into our hearts by the Holy Spirit which has been given us. We were still helpless when at his appointed moment Christ died for sinful men. It is not easy to die even for a good man – though of course for someone really worthy, a man might be prepared to die – but what proves that God loves us is that Christ died for us while we were still sinners. Having died to make us righteous, is it likely that he would now fail to save us from God's anger? When we were reconciled to God by the death of his Son, we were still enemies; now that we have been reconciled, surely we may count on being saved by the life of his Son? Not merely because we have been reconciled but because we are filled with joyful trust in God, through our Lord Jesus Christ, through whom we have already gained our reconciliation.

Romans 5:5-11

IDENTIFYING OBSTACLES

- Does my baptism still have meaning?

- Can others see in me qualities or gifts that reflect the Holy Spirit? Are my gifts life-giving or do I use them selfishly?

- Am I consistent in my baptismal commitment?

REFLECTION

Walking down the sand dunes towards the sparkling waters of the local seashore on a calm day stirs up personal reflections on my baptism. When the pure, silver suds of the tide gently gush towards me, I think of the waters poured over me at baptism. The warm breeze blanketing the seashore feels like the breath of the Holy Spirit wrapping me forever in God's love. When climbing back up the sand dunes, I always praise God for his legacy of lasting love that has come down the ages to me. I am also reminded anew of the calling of God in my life.

We are familiar with the word legacy. We think of the legacy received by us from our families: the love, the fostering of positive values and outlook in life, the sacrifice and commitment stimulating our growth and development. Unfortunately, for some the family legacy might be one of insecurity, bitterness or sadness. From school days there is the legacy of education and friends, and maybe some embittering memories too. From our country we inherit a standard of living, basic human rights and freedom of speech; whereas in some countries it might be an inheritance of poverty, inequality and corruption.

Our culture gives us our familial and societal values and respect for rules, legislation and government. Some cultures have done untold harm, for example, by the glorification of violence and excessive dependence on alcohol. From Jesus Christ too we have received a legacy. It is a legacy of love, which has been borne across the ages to us. It is the gift of his love, the gift of eternal life.

Saint Paul says that the 'love of God has been poured into our hearts by the Holy Spirit' at baptism. What proves that God loves us is that Jesus, his Son, 'died for us while we were still sinners'. God was not waiting for us to gain reconciliation by our own means. It is through his death that Jesus washed away the inheritance of sin in order for us to become reconciled with God and to pass from this life into new life in heaven.

Baptism connects us to God through the Holy Spirit and, therefore, we belong to the family of God – all beloved sons and daughters of our heavenly Father. God lives in us. Our baptism then invites us to take up the duty of responsibility and neighbourliness to one another. When we stand on the shores of heaven, we hope that others will have felt the better for having known us. We pray that we will leave the fingerprints of God's love after us in acts such as kindness, generosity and works of mercy, forgivness, peace and joy. The healing love God gives to us in baptism is the same healing love God wants us to give to others. God is present in us through the Holy Spirit, empowering us to do good work. Those to whom we pass on Christ's legacy of love and good work will, therefore, give the praise to our Father in heaven.

A Personal Response

- Take a moment to reflect on what it means for you to be called a child of God.

- Use your gifts and qualities more effectively for the benefit of others.

- Pray through the Holy Spirit that God may be more operative in your work.

- Think of people who have passed on the legacy of Christ's love to you and helped you to grow in the Spirit of God and pray a prayer for them.

A Prayer for the Journey

Loving Lord, source of life,

I thank you for the legacy of your love, the gift of eternal life.
I am grateful to those who helped to pass on your love from down the ages and which has been handed on to me by my parents and my community.
Through the gift of the Spirit in me, help me to continue passing on your legacy of love to others.
May I never be so preoccupied with my own interests as to ignore the needs of my fellow pilgrims in baptism.

I pray through Jesus Christ, Our Lord. Amen.

ROCK OF SUPPORT

> He got into the boat followed by his disciples. Without warning a storm broke over the lake, so violent that the waves were breaking right over the boat. But he was asleep. So they went to him and woke him saying, 'Save us Lord we are going down!' And he said to them, 'Why are you so frightened, you men of little faith?' And with that he stood up and rebuked the winds and the sea; and all was calm again. The men were astounded and said, 'Whatever kind of man is this? Even the winds obey him'.
>
> *Matthew 8:23-27*

Identifying Obstacles

- Am I patient with God in times of crisis? Do I trust God enough to take me through the storm?

- Do I react angrily instead of asking God for courage to overcome or to accept a turbulent experience?

- Have I been a rock to others, especially to those who needed me? Have I been supportive, reliable and trustworthy?

REFLECTION

For thousands of years the rock has stared out from its sturdy abode on the sea face. In these years, the rock has felt the furious cacophony of the white unruly tide against its innocent face. In these years too, the rock has known the shimmering tide's silver waves along its rugged face. Whatever the ocean's mood, the rock always embraced it.

There is a comparison with our own lives to that of the rock on the sea face. On our journey to heaven the waves of life, under its varying guises, splash continuously against us. We enjoy the softness of life's waves when our plans are undisturbed and when life is good. Then when the harshness of these waves comes crashing against us (when well-organised plans do not work out; when it is a bad day at work; when all barriers of communication collapse in relationships or friendships; or when there is personal tragedy), we no longer feel as self-assured. Our peace of mind is disturbed by the waves of anxiety and annoyance. When the stormy waves of life swirl around us we may not be as sure of God's presence anymore or be as steadfast in our faith.

When we feel that the waves are breaking 'right over the boat' of our lives, we might think we are powerless like the apostles. Like them, our cries to God might be: 'Are you asleep?' 'Do you care about what is happening to me?' 'Are you listening?' 'Save me Lord'. Trying to embrace these stormy waves may appear impossible at first. It is strengthening and encouraging to read about people or listen to them on radio programmes, or meet them in the community describing how they learned to cope with tragedy or personal problems in their lives. They may claim God helped them to embrace these furious waves that threatened to turn the boat of their lives upside down. Through the support of loved ones and close friends, and invoking the presence of God through prayer, they felt the power of God within them touching the turmoil in their lives, eventually bringing calmness and stability to their hearts. God was ever-present 'in the boat' with them.

God calls us not to be frightened when the stormy waves of life swirl around us. He wants us to know that he is ever-present, even though we might not be aware of his closeness. He asks us not to lack faith in his presence in times of crisis. With the help of the Spirit of God, we will weather the storm and remain steady in the face of the adversities that life may bring.

A Personal Response

- Think of the people who have been a rock to you. Return their kindness.

- Think of support groups in your area that might be a rock for you. Find out more information about them. Do not be afraid to reach out to them.

- Make time and space for God in prayer to give you guidance and strength to lead you through turbulent moments on your journey.

A Prayer for the Journey

Loving Lord,

Thank you for your loving presence, which helps me to steer through the storms of life.

In the way you calmed the stormy waters when you were in the boat with the apostles, calm whatever fear and anxiety there is in me, restoring courage and inner peace. May my faith be strong enough to reassure me of your caring and loving presence.

Thank you for those who blessed me with their loving, healing words and actions and who have been a lasting rock for me.

I pray through Jesus Christ, Our Lord. Amen.

RECALLING STORYTELLING

> In all this Jesus spoke to the crowds in parables;
> indeed, he would never speak to them except in
> parables. This was to fulfill the prophecy:
>   'I will speak to you in parables and expound things
> hidden since the foundation of the world.'
>   *Matthew 13:34-35*

IDENTIFYING OBSTACLES

- What story has made a powerful impact on me?

- Did I spread malicious stories? Did they damage
  someone's reputation?

- Have I been on the receiving end of malicious stories?

REFLECTION

He stood stationary, a man at peace with the world, with
himself and with his Creator. The windows in his red,
galvanised cottage were like two small eyes always on duty
serenely watching the world. The door was of two halves;
the top half opened in welcome. An oil lamp, suspended

from the low ceiling on a special hook, gave a gentle glow of light on a dark winter's night. The neighbours' visits and the small black battery radio kept him up-to-date with the happenings of the world. The flickering coal embers in the open-hearth fireplace on a winter's night often poked his memory bank, which stored many old stories that would suddenly come alive when neighbours called. The humorous and sometimes sad stories that filed out of his memory bank shuttled the imagination of his listeners into the world of his youth. An encore of laughter, wrapped in nostalgia, warmly interrupted each story as he sat ensconced on his old, brown armchair. When his soul eventually ascended from his tired and frail body, his world still existed in his stories, eternalised in the memory of his listening neighbours.

Stories bring the past to life. Books stored in libraries record happenings and events around the world for their new readers. In local communities, stories of interest are passed on from person to person, or recorded, preserving their past. Stories define a community and a nation.

Jesus was a storyteller. Through stories he wanted to reveal God the Father's love for his people and 'expound things hidden since the foundation of the world'. Jesus 'would never speak to them except in parables' – he was not on the entertainment circuit earning money telling stories. He left his secure job as a carpenter to travel to the villages and towns telling stories about God's compassionate love for his people. In the synagogues, on the hill tops, on street corners, people flocked to listen to him talk passionately about God's salvation for his people.

His stories helped them to open their minds to the ways of God and called them to conversion: to renounce their sins, to change from their old ways of living and to structure their lives on his teachings. Jesus told these stories with excitement, enthusiasm and love.

In between telling these stories, Jesus lived them. He did not merely bombard his listeners with stories about the Kingdom of Heaven; they came alive in his actions. He acted compassionately and he healed those who came for healing. He forgave those who sought forgiveness. His love was inclusive. People flocked to listen to him. Eventually his stories about God's love and forgiveness brought him to the cross, which was the greatest proof of God's inclusive love for his people. The stories of Jesus bring the landscape of God's Kingdom to life when we listen to them and open our hearts in welcome.

A Personal Response

- Share stories that are fulfilling, inspirational and uplifting.

- Choose a story from Jesus' teachings that had the greatest personal impact on you.

- Think of some area of your life in which you might find healing through reflecting on this story.

- If you belong to a prayer group, perhaps use this story for reflection with the group. Others too might find inspiration and spiritual nourishment from it.

A Prayer for the Journey

Loving Lord,

Thank you for revealing your Father's compassionate and healing love for me in your stories.
Open me to the wonder of this life in your stories. I pray that your stories will come alive in me today and that I will recreate for others the landscape of your love.

I pray through Jesus Christ, Our Lord. Amen.

A SMOOTH JOURNEY

> Make no mistake about this, it is all that is good, everything that is perfect, which is given us from above; it comes down from the Father of all light; with him there is no such thing as alteration, no shadow of a change. By his own choice he made us his own children by the message of the truth so that we should be a sort of first-fruits of all that he created.
>
> *James 1:16-18*

IDENTIFYING OBSTACLES

- Is my spiritual journey smooth?
- Is God blamed for something that has gone wrong in my life at present?
- Do I blame others?

REFLECTION

Learning to cycle for the first time can be a bruising experience for some. Before co-ordination and balance skills are discovered, there is always the risk of falling off the bicycle and hurting yourself. With the support and encouragement of loved ones, you persevere until you discover the art of cycling. Some might be proud of their wounds and see in them their sense of achievement.

We experience a similiar rite of passage in other areas of life. There is the journey from the turbulent teens towards developing a more self-assured, confident existence. The first few months in a new school or college bring feelings of uncertainty for some until they integrate into their new surroundings. Some people claim that a year or more passed before they settled into their new place of employment. It is common for people to suffer inner turmoil in accepting themselves for who and what they are, or just trying to be at ease in their own skin and accepting their lot in life. For relationships to mature, it takes time to accept weaknesses and strengths, likes and dislikes.

When we talk about growing in God's love, many also experience trials. There are moments in life when we doubt God's loving presence. Some vent their anger towards God in times of trouble: 'Why did God allow this tragedy to happen?' 'Does God not care?' Disillusionment then erodes our faith in God. Sometimes the pain of spiritual growth casts God to one side, as if in some way God caused this pain. When physical pain occurs, generally something is blamed for it. During personal and emotional trauma the inclination is to apportion blame to God. In this situation God appears not to care. Naturally, we grapple with our pain of spiritual growth –

growing in the love of God. Initially, the reaction towards God is anger that he should seem so uncaring. It is often said that it is in these volatile situations that we really come face-to-face with God. God does not mind those angry emotions taken out on him – that is also prayer. However, anger towards God is a heavy burden to carry.

It is inspiring to listen to or read stories about people who said that at the beginning they vented their anger at God when confronted with great pain, such as personal loss or despair. Now that they have moved on a little, they realise that it was God who took them through the pain. One person claimed that her personal tragedy forced her to re-evaluate her life and to reflect more deeply on the meaning of life. Thankfully for her she is, to use her own words, 'closer to God now than she was before the pain of her tragedy'. She asserts now that God did not cause the pain. She might agree that her personal tragedy transformed her outlook in life in a very positive way. Sometimes it is the personal pain that inspires us to re-evaluate life and to see beyond the hurt. It is said that sometimes you have to lose God to find him again.

We are told 'all that is good, everything that is perfect, which is given us' comes down from heaven. Bad things do not come from heaven. God is love and he only wishes us good; he does not inflict bad or harmful things on us. These words inspire us to let go of the burden of anger towards God, for whatever reason we might feel it, and continue to grow in God's love for us.

A Personal Response

- Instead of merely being angry and blaming God for something bad in your life, why not look for group solidarity and cohesion in your family and in your community? God's help is also present in those people.

- Take a step back from your grievance to reflect if God really caused your pain.

- Keeping in mind God's unconditional love for you, ask God to help you through your pain.

- Pray in the Spirit of God for the courage to reach out and look for help.

- This might be an opportunity to deepen your understanding of God's love for you.

A Prayer for the Journey

Loving Lord,

All that is good and perfect which is given to me comes down from heaven. You are a God of love who never stops loving me.

Through your love for me and with the support and love of others, take away any anger I may have towards you. Transform my anger into peace and sensitivity so as to deepen my relationship with you and others. I thank you for giving me people who are channels of your divine love.

I pray through Jesus Christ, Our Lord. Amen.

THE BEAUTY WITHIN

The scribes and Pharisees brought a woman along who had been caught committing adultery; and making her stand there in full view of everybody, they said to Jesus, 'Master, this woman was caught in the very act of committing adultery, and Moses has ordered us in the Law to condemn women like this to death by stoning. What have you to say?' They asked him this as a test, looking for something to use against him. But Jesus bent down and started writing on the ground with his finger. As they persisted with their question, he looked up and said, 'If there is one of you who has not sinned, let him be the first to throw a stone at her'. Then he bent down and wrote on the ground again. When they heard this they went away one by one, beginning with the eldest, until Jesus was left alone with the woman, who remained standing there. He looked up and said, 'Woman, where are they? Has no one condemned you?' 'No one, sir,' she replied. 'Neither do I condemn you,' said Jesus, 'go away, and don't sin any more.'

John 8:3-11

IDENTIFYING OBSTACLES

- Does rejection cause me to feel undervalued or excluded? How does this affect me?

- Do I feel rejected because I do not or cannot live up to other people's expectations of me?

- Do I undermine others when they are downtrodden or because they do not live up to my expectations?

REFLECTION

Transporting a three-ton block of marble was difficult in the sixteenth century, so when some artists rejected the block of marble – because it had a flaw, or it was not perfectly white throughout – the hauliers were not going to take it back to the quarry; instead, they brought it down the street to Michelangelo's studio. Michelangelo did not refuse it. The blue streak in it presented a serious challenge, but he decided to try to work with it. When he produced the famous statue of David, the blue streak appeared like a vein beneath the skin; he had turned the fault into an asset. Michelangelo is supposed to have said that David was waiting to come out of the marble.

Just as Michelanglo saw the good and potential in the flawed block of marble, God sees the good in each person, despite their flaws and failures. We know from the Gospels that Jesus sees through flaws and recognises the good among the outcasts, the sinners, the downtrodden, the drug addicts and the undervalued. Jesus saw beyond the reputation of the woman caught in adultery to the goodness within her. The people who took her to Jesus wanted her to die because of her sins – Jesus asks her to die to her sins. Jesus does not question her about her past but gently says, 'Go away and don't sin any more'. He acknowledges that she has sinned, while at the same time he helps her to see beyond her past towards the goodnees that he sees in her. He restores her self-worth, and perhaps for the first time in her life she feels valued. It is the overwhelming love and compassion she experiences through her brief encounter with Jesus that changes her life forever. Jesus helped her to discover in herself the beauty and goodness that was waiting to come out. The people condemned her past and wanted to end her life. Jesus healed her past and offered her a new beginning.

Jesus does no less for us. Regardless of our past, he does not push us away or reject us when we come to him. His only desire is to love us back from our sins. The love Jesus has for the woman people wanted to stone is the same love he has for us. Jesus wants us to learn about God's love through him. God's wish is also for us to discover the potential for goodness that he can see in us. Whatever our faults and flaws may be, God offers us a new beginning. His love conquers our past sins. God does not spend time dwelling on our past sins, but if we allow him, we can become a vehicle for his love to others in the world.

A Personal Response

- Take a moment to reflect on the positive qualities God sees in you – name them.

- Ask God to help you change a habit or a quality which will enable you to become a better person.

- Think of a way that the attitude of Jesus can help you to see beyond the faults of someone you dislike.

- Give an encouraging word to someone that will make them feel more valued.

A Prayer for the Journey

Loving Lord,

Conqueror of sins,
No one is pushed away or rejected because they have sinned.
Your love reaches out to everyone regardless of their faults and sins.
Help me to change old ways, old habits that are soul destructive.
May your unconditional love for me inspire me to see beyond my faults and the faults of others to the goodness in all of us.

I pray through Jesus Christ, Our Lord. Amen.

STOPPING AT THE FORGIVENESS CROSSROADS

> From the depths I call to you, Yahweh,
> Lord, listen to my cry for help!
> Listen compassionately to my pleading!
>
> If you never overlooked our sins, Yahweh,
> Lord, could anyone survive?
> But you do forgive us:
> and for that we revere you.
>
> I wait for Yahweh, my soul waits for him,
> I rely on his promise,
> my soul relies on the Lord
> more than a watchman on the coming of dawn.
>
> Let Israel rely on Yahweh
> as much as the watchman on the dawn!
> For it is with Yahweh that mercy is to be found,
> and a generous redemption;
> it is he who redeems Israel from all their sins.
> *Psalm 130*

Identifying Obstacles

- Do I ever doubt God's forgiveness?

- Have I committed a sin that I judge to be beyond God's mercy?

- Am I inclined to judge myself in the past with what I know now through hindsight?

Reflection

'Will God forgive me?' or 'Is it possible for God to forgive me?' – some people ask these questions when they have seriously sinned. A beautiful approach to the question of God's forgiveness is to encourage such people to ask, 'What lengths does God go to to forgive me?' One way to answer this question is to spend some time reflecting before the crucifix of Christ. From his pierced side and the holes in his hands and feet flows the beautiful fragrance of forgiveness that washes our sins away. His thin, outstretched arms lovingly embrace us in our sinfulness, and forgiveness spills down his furrowed face healing our sinful wounds. He wears on his head our crown of sins and places on our heads his crown of forgiveness.

Jesus does not hold onto our past mistakes and spend his time adding up our faults: 'If you never overlooked our sins, Lord, could anyone survive? But you do forgive us: and for that we revere you.' Jesus downloads forgiveness into our lives and gives us a new updated program for living. The Lord helps us work with our sins and to see through them and move beyond them. It is often said that the way a person deals with victory says something about his character, but how he copes with defeat says even more about him. On the cross it appeared that Jesus' mission failed, yet in his great agony he prayed for forgiveness for those who condemned him to this fate. Later his friends realised the cross was not a failure but a victory over sin, and the resurrection gave witness to that.

It is through the victory of the cross over sin and death that God provides us with a new program, which helps us to deal with our sins in the light of the cross. We can make a choice to lament and condemn ourselves to our past sins and stay there. Self-condemnation at least reflects sorrow for the sins of the past. Why not also move on, then, to the next stage of sorrow and accept the forgiveness Jesus offers us from the cross? It says something about our character that we, with Jesus, are able to work with our sins and past mistakes and to see beyond them to what Jesus is offering us. By accepting Jesus' forgiveness, we can move towards reconciliation and become better people.

Thank God for his forgiveness in the sure and absolute knowledge that God's forgiveness reaches out to anyone who asks for it. Jesus died on the cross so that our sins will be forgiven. Yes, God forgives us; God never stops forgiving us. Jesus came from heaven to tell us about God's forgiveness, even if that meant dying on the cross for us: 'For it is with Yahweh that mercy is to be found, and a generous redemption.' 'It is he,' the Psalmist says, who will redeem us from all our sins.

A Personal Response

- If the Sacrament of Reconciliation is a difficulty for you, why not think of a compassionate confessor to whom you can go and confess your sin.

- If you do not know a confessor too well, visit a reconciliation centre where you can meet a confessor.

- Imagine the peace of mind God is offering you when you confess your 'unforgivable sin'.

A Prayer for the Journey

Loving Lord,

Full of compassion and forgiver of sins, you do not hold my sins against me when I come to you asking for forgiveness, even when I think my sins are unforgivable.

Help me to confess my sins to you in the Sacrament of Reconciliation, regardless of how unforgivable I think those sins are.

Give me the grace and belief to accept your forgiveness in my life, using it as a way forward to work through my wrongdoing and to continue on my journey in the joyful knowledge that I am forgiven.

I pray through Jesus Christ, Our Lord. Amen.

HELP ME TO FORGIVE MYSELF

SCRIPTURE

> At that instant, while he was still speaking, the
> cock crew, and the Lord turned and looked straight
> at Peter, and Peter remembered what the Lord had
> said to him, 'Before the cock crows today, you will
> have disowned me three times'. And he went
> outside and wept bitterly.
>
> *Luke 22:60-62*

IDENTIFYING OBSTACLES

- Am I constantly regurgitating and reliving hurtful
  events?

- Can I identify the sources of my inner conflict?

- Am I missing out on new opportunities as a result of
  not letting go of deep-set anxieties?

REFLECTION

'I cannot forgive myself,' people often say. They are very disappointed with what they have done and suffer pain of regret thinking about what they did. They are aware of God's forgiveness, yet they find that forgiving themselves is difficult. Much of their time is spent dealing with the inner torment of their sins, dwelling on them constantly and repeatedly going over them in their minds. Remembering our sins can lead us into overindulging our feelings of shame and guilt, which greatly disturb our peace of mind. Some people condemn themselves for a long time because of the wrong they did in the past. Self-hatred festers like bacteria in them, impacting hugely on their health and well-being.

The example of Peter forgiving himself and working through his past mistakes provides us with a way of working towards self-forgiveness. When he denied knowing Jesus, he knew his relationship with Jesus was strong enough to withstand what he did. When Jesus 'looked straight at Peter', guilt darkened his eyes: 'He went outside and wept bitterly.' Tears of shame and sorrow engulfed him. 'How can I forgive myself?' he thought, but he refused to allow the feelings of guilt to gnaw away at him forever. Peter forgave himself because he knew Jesus well enough to know that he would not hold it against him. Nowhere did Jesus say to Peter, 'I will never forget those times you denied me'. Jesus was not interested in what Peter did wrong in the past because he had plans for him – plans to continue his mission.

Self-forgiveness is difficult for some people and guilty feelings linger for years. We constantly wish that we could rewind to the moment when we did wrong and amend it. Since we know we cannot go back in time and correct our sins, why give so much valuable time and energy over to the things we did wrong? Instead, we should use our time reflecting on what Jesus is offering us now. Guilty feelings can be good in that they help us acknowledge that we have done wrong and, therefore, humble us before the Lord. But what good is it if our constant focus on our guilt prevents us from truly accepting the Lord's forgiveness? Peter was humble enough to accept his mistakes before the Lord and to move forward in God's love and forgiveness.

Peter's example invites us to go forward. God's love for us is so powerful that it overcomes our faults and mistakes. As soon as we forgive ourselves for our sins so as to fully allow God's forgiveness flood our hearts, we can begin to feel God's peace replacing the feelings of guilt. God has plans for us to follow. Imagine how much of God's work would have been left undone if Peter refused to forgive himself. Imagine too all the good work that would be left undone if we used so much precious time condemning ourselves to our past mistakes. All that remains for us is to accept God's forgiveness fully by forgiving the sins in us and continuing to do the work of God.

A Personal Response

- Accept that you cannot undo the sins of the past. Make a firm decision that you will forgive yourself. Imagine how Jesus might be asking you to do so.

- Once you have acknowledged your sin and celebrated confession, move forward. Then say a prayer thanking and accepting God's forgiveness for you.

- Think of something you might do to celebrate this moment of self-forgiveness.

A Prayer for the Journey

God our heavenly Father,

You do not waste time dwelling on my past sins. Your non-judgemental approach to Peter empowered him to become a humble instrument in your plan of salvation for the world.

You do not want me to go on lamenting about my past but to look to the good I can do for you in the future. Help me to accept myself more and to allow your gift of forgiveness to liberate myself from my guilt.

I pray through Jesus Christ, Our Lord. Amen.

SUPPORTING THE HEALING PROCESS

SCRIPTURE

> When they reached the place called The Skull, they crucified him there and the two criminals also, one on the right, the other on the left. Jesus said, 'Father forgive them; they do not know what they are doing'. Then they cast lots to share out his clothing.
> *Luke 23:33-34*

IDENTIFYING OBSTACLES

- Do I have old wounds that still disturb me and my peace with God?

- Do I hold grudges?

- Does failure to treat an old wound such as resentment or revenge present itself as an obstacle to inner peace?

REFLECTION

If a physical wound is not treated quickly, efficiently and appropriately, it will fester over time. Consequently, there is the horrid fear that damage will encamp permanently in that area of the body. The toxins need to be released in order to restore flexibility and freedom to the damaged area and repel the invading pain. This requires targeting the root of the problem, and the rebuilding and fortifying of the area that needs healing.

As with the human body, the human spirit can also be hurt. The irritation from emotional and spiritual bruises, which can emerge to the surface, also deserves attention, so as to help the process of removing the toxins from the soul. To deal with the pain caused by these bruises requires getting to the root of the problem. It means attending to the hurt rather than ignoring it. Otherwise, anger, bitterness, hate and other destructive emotions may build up in our hearts. The support of others – a family member, a trustworthy friend, a spiritual healer or someone adept in this area of work – is a necessary help in dealing with old wounds, which painfully persist in the undergrowth of our hearts. Otherwise, the poison of old hurts remain and emit toxins, such as anger or the inability to forgive. Subsequently, our way to peace of mind is blocked; our way to God's peace is impeded.

Healing a wound inflicted on us by others is challenging. Jesus offers us his way of letting go – the way of forgiveness. Jesus not only preached forgiveness, he also practised it. On the cross, while he was being mocked and taunted, he shouted out with all the strength he could find within himself at that moment: 'Father forgive them, they do not know what they are doing.' Jesus had every reason to fill his heart with bitterness and revenge, but he chose the way of forgiveness. It is in this same spirit that Jesus asks us to follow his example. Forgiveness is the ideal way for spiritual growth.

By living the process of forgiveness and seeking the right support and careful guidance, the wounds and sores will begin to fade. A sports injury does not go away in a single treatment. The pain is more easily subdued if it is followed by a succession of treatments over a required period of time, and the recommended physical exercises are done appropriately. Reconciliation with the pain of the past is also a process we must work at over time.

When Jesus said, 'Father forgive them', all human sins were included also. Forgiveness is God's wonderful gift to us through his Son, Jesus. A good starting point to begin the process of forgiveness is to spend some time reflecting on God's unconditional love and forgiveness for us, no matter how often we disappoint him. Once the sense of God's forgiveness grows within us, we may find that we are also growing in forgiveness for others.

A Personal Response

- Identify an old wound that requires treatment. Ask the Lord to work with you towards peace and healing.

- Would talking to someone help the journey of healing?

- Recall a time when you sought forgiveness. Did it restore inner peace?

- Over a period of time, do your best to extend God's forgiveness towards someone who you find difficult to forgive.

A Prayer for the Journey

Loving Lord, full of mercy,

From the cross you forgave your accusers their sins and you did not hold bitterness or resentment in your heart towards them. You also forgave me my sins at that moment.

Where there are feelings of anger or resentment simmering in me, give me your help to heal these energy-draining feelings by transforming them into peace and forgiveness. May peace and forgiveness grow in my heart each day so that I can feel your peace and forgiveness surround me.

I pray through Jesus Christ, Our Lord. Amen.

CRYSTAL CLEAR

SCRIPTURE

> For us, our homeland is in heaven, and from heaven comes the saviour we are waiting for, the Lord Jesus Christ, and he will transfigure these wretched bodies of ours into copies of his glorious body. He will do that by the same power with which he can subdue the whole universe. So then, my dear friends do not give way but remain faithful in the Lord.
> *Philippians 3:20-4:1*

IDENTIFYING OBSTACLES

- What does heaven mean to me?
- Can I prepare for life after death?
- Is life for me too focused on materialistic things?

REFLECTION

A free-flowing river peacefully winds its way through the countryside like a pilgrim on a journey. Even though sometimes its beautiful, crystal-clear water is discoloured by sliding clay from its embankment or on occasion finds its path obstructed by what nature discards, the water of the river always gushes forward, purifying itself in the process. Whatever trouble it encounters, the river seems determined to find a way to continue on its journey until it reaches its destination and falls into the embracing arms of the ocean.

We are pilgrims on a journey to heaven. Many times our way to heaven is perhaps impeded by greed, suffering, bitter memories and jealousy, which causes us to lose our way and stray in other directions. Our own outlook in life may focus more on the things of earth, such as, 'I want to accumulate more money' or 'I am too busy or too tired to go to Church'. If we have moved away from God and lost sight of the things of heaven, it is necessary that we reawaken the spiritual side of ourselves and then pay more attention to God's call to reconciliation.

The qualities of life in heaven are no different from the best qualities of life now: love, peace, joy, gentleness, faithfulness and self-control. We are called to these qualities even now, not only by others who need them from us, but also by God, who planted the seeds of those qualities in us. Heaven is not a destination of the future; it is something we can bring about even now. If we are serious about doing that and there are obstacles on our path, whether we or others have put them there, the Sacrament of Reconciliation offers us the opportunity to work towards moving these obstacles. The Sacrament of Reconciliation is a celebration of God's healing love for us right here, right now. This sacrament is God's gift to us to assist us and redirect us to heaven if we have lost our way. It offers us the chance to begin afresh, to evaluate our life and to reconnect with God. Regardless of what we have done, or what shame or guilt we may carry within, the Lord welcomes us to celebrate his healing love for us in this sacrament. The God of the Gospel waits patiently for us to come to him.

In the Sacrament of Reconciliation, we try to leave behind our old sinful ways with a desire to change, thus getting back on the path to heaven. God gives us the power to change and to renew our relationship with him. We allow God to transform us into 'copies of his own glorious body'. After we celebrate the sacrament, we thank and praise God in prayer for his healing love and for giving us the grace to change: 'Our homeland is in Heaven', where 'Jesus will transform these wretched bodies of ours into copies of his own glorious body'.

A Personal Response

- Take some quiet time to think of any changes you need to make in your lifestyle, which will help you on your journey to heaven.

- Reflect on the way you presently use the gifts of this world. Might there be a way to better use them, without exploiting them?

- Invest energy in working for the 'things of heaven'.

- If you have strayed off God's path on your spiritual journey, begin again by celebrating the Sacrament of Reconciliation. In this healing sacrament God increases his strength in you to remove any obstacles that may exist between you and heaven.

A Prayer for the Journey

Loving Lord,

You want to include me in your everlasting love in heaven.

Even when I stray from the path to you, you do not reject me but you desire that I change my ways when I do not cultivate the deeds of goodness you have placed in me. You want me to appreciate and enjoy wisely the gifts of this life, but not to exploit them such that they might lead me away from you.

With your help, may I not become obsessed with material things that might side-track me on my journey. May my faith always be strong so that earthly temptations will not lead me astray.

I ask the Holy Spirit to be my light, to guard and rule me and to guide me to heaven.

I pray through Jesus Christ, Our Lord. Amen.

DIFFUSING A
TURBULENT MEMORY

SCRIPTURE

> Peace I bequeath to you, my own peace I give you,
> a peace the world cannot give, this is my gift to you.
> Do not let your hearts be troubled or afraid ... And
> yet I am not alone, because the Father is with me. I
> have told you all this so that you may find peace in
> me. In the world you will have trouble, but be brave:
> I have conquered the world.
>
> *John 14:27, 16:32-33*

IDENTIFYING OBSTACLES

- What consequences do my painful memories have on
  my relationships with people in my life today?

- Have I noticed any symptoms or signs that painful
  memories affect my health, my peace of mind?

- Do they make inroads in my relationship with God?
  How?

REFLECTION

Imagine that while walking you trip and fall over an obstacle lying on the ground. You lift yourself up again from where you fell. If you injure yourself as a result of the fall, it is wise to care for the injury first. Then continue, perhaps slowly at first, but eventually gathering greater momentum until you reach your destination. When working through a painful memory, wishing for it to heal, the place to begin is at the cause of the hurt and not somewhere else.

Some people carry the pain of past memories for a long time, in some cases even forever. From listening to people's experiences, it seems that a painful, lingering memory can cripple their self-worth and self-esteem. This memory invades their peace of mind, leaving a trail of turmoil behind, resulting in low energy, poor sleep patterns and in some cases depression. They wish that this hurt could be erased forever. If you damage your car or watch or radio, you bring it to a repair shop. When a hurtful memory damages us in some way, the words of Jesus encourage us to turn to God our Creator for help and healing. If you should damage your watch by accidently letting it fall, it is not the watchmaker's fault, but the watchmaker can restore it again. Without God's presence or perspective, the painful memory can weigh in us permanently, such that feelings of worthlessness can consume us, sapping most of our energy. Opening our hearts to receive the peace of God increases our capacity to be more Christ-centered in our outlook, and to grow more liberated from the pain the past may have inflicted on us.

In God's presence and with his perspective we can begin to do something with these feelings. Jesus shows us his way. In his darkest hour Jesus says to us: 'And yet I am not alone, because my Father is with me. I have told you this so that you may find peace in me.' Jesus knows that we will have trouble in life and that we will be hurt. That is why he says: 'Peace I bequeath to you, my own peace I give you. Do not let your hearts be troubled or afraid.' Jesus suffered many bad memories – the lies told about him, the desertion of his friends at the most difficult time in his life, the vicious taunts and hateful words hurled at him when he was carrying his cross and then the crucifixion itself. He had plenty of excuses to fill his heart with bitterness and anger, but instead he knew that 'the Father is with me' and he gave these hurts over to him.

The peace Jesus achieved with his Father during those moments is the same peace into which he wants to lead us. Jesus knows the difficult challenge of moving forward when we are hurt, yet he wants us to get on with living our lives. It does not mean that the wound will go away; Jesus still carries the scars of his troubles yet he is at peace with them. The peace Jesus experienced with the Father strengthened him in his mission. Jesus offers us this peace as a way forward in coping with our distress. His peace in us will help to soften the pain we experience so that it will not consume us completely. Jesus' way offers us a new perspective for dealing with a bad memory while bringing calmness and peace with it. He offers us his way as a process of overcoming the pain to achieve a greater harmony in our lives. In this way, we gain a greater capacity to experience the same peace Jesus enjoys with the Father.

A Personal Response

- Spend a few moments listening to your feelings, then share them with God. Leave yourself open to God's inspiration, which will help you.

- Share the burden of your hurt with God (through the Sacrament of Reconciliation or by seeking support through a person or group).

- Follow the example of Jesus our Saviour in sharing your pain with God our Father.

A Prayer for the Journey

Loving Lord,

You shared your pain with God our Father as you continued to enjoy his peace in you.
Give me the strength to give over to you the memories that burden my peace and cause conflict in me. Give me the grace to be at peace with such memories through the guidance of your Spirit and the spirit of others.

I pray through Jesus Christ, Our Lord. Amen.

RESTORING YOUR GOOD NAME

Scripture

> I say this to you: love your enemies and pray for those who persecute you; so that you may be children of your father in heaven; for he makes his sun rise on the evil and on the good, and sends rain on the just and on the unjust. For if you love those who love you, what reward have you? Do not even tax collectors do the same? And if you salute only one of your brethren, what more are you doing than others? Do not even the Gentiles do the same? You, therefore, must be perfect, as your heavenly Father is perfect.
>
> *Matthew 5:44-48*

Identifying Obstacles

- How have I encountered untruths or hurtful gossip? How is it affecting my inner peace? Is it affecting me today?

- Does waiting for an opportunity for revenge motivate me?

- Am I able to forgive like Jesus? How do I react to that? Does it concern me in any way?

REFLECTION

To be a victim of idle gossip, slander or lies is a very damaging and deflating experience. It is something that pains you, gnawing away at your inner peace, often resulting in stress-related illnesses. A good reputation and a good name is something to which everyone is entitled. When your reputation is attacked, undermined in some way or destroyed by innacurate reports or by false accusations, the feeling can be one of absolute despair. It is like a virus invading your peace of mind. In some cases it is necessary to go through the painful process of confronting the offenders in court or by asking them to stop their malicious slander. You do all within your rights to prevent lies escalating and to restore your good character. Even when your reputation has been restored, damage has been done. You still suffer its effect for some time, maybe a lifetime. We have little power over what others think of us, but we at least have power over our own feelings.

This human experience is also the human experience of Jesus. We can see how Jesus dealt with it. Jesus was an innocent victim too – he was crucified as a criminal. The religious leaders incited hatred for him among the people by filling them with treacherous lies. Jesus sought neither revenge nor retaliation. Earlier in his preaching he told the people to 'love your enemies' and to 'pray for those who persecute you'. This is the path Jesus chose when dealing with those who vilified him.

We are pushed to the very limits of our love and forgiveness when Jesus asks us to love and pray for those who have damaged us severely. This is very challenging, perhaps even disturbing for some. We might initially think it impossible to achieve; it takes time. At first the inclination might be towards revenge, to wish our offenders the worst and to seek opportunities for payback. Jesus knows where we are coming from. Yet wanting revenge on our offenders will probably add more distress to our already damaged inner peace. Jesus knows that revenge in the long-term will only add more to our woes.

Choosing to forgive in this situation is answering the call of God. We may think this is not achievable at first. The inability to forgive may cause us frustration because we are basically good people and we have a good sense of God in the greater part of our lives. To be trapped in this pain creates a feeling of powerlessness, which can cause tension. There is an honourable way of dealing with it. Jesus wants us to reflect on how he dealt with the problem of lies and false accusations in his life; he offers us an honourable and noble way. Difficult as it may seem, Jesus wants us to follow his way of reconciliation, which involves trusting that Jesus knows what is good for us. This does not mean that we will send our offenders greetings at Christmas, but we can pray for God to heal them. We can pray that they may not become stuck in sin or that their potential for goodness may not be corroded further by hardness of heart, and that they may become free from wrongdoing. Do keep in mind that the Spirit of God dwells in us, and that by responding to the Spirit we will be helped to move forward, towards reconciliation. When those who are familiar with our painful experiences see that we are making an effort to forgive those who have done their worst to us, they will see God at work. Through us, then, the Spirit of God's love and forgiveness might help others to act in the same compassionate way under similar circumstances.

A Personal Response

- Talk to the people who can help you with the damage done to you because of lies: a close friend, a mediator or a spiritual director.

- Do not recall what happened to you at every opportunity. To continue on your spiritual journey, it is good to let rest what happened to you, otherwise you will remain a prisoner to your pain.

- Say a prayer for all innocent people who have been accused in the wrong, especially those in prisons throughout the world.

A Prayer for the Journey

Loving Lord,

You loved your enemies and you prayed for them from the cross asking forgiveness for them.

Help me to choose the way of forgiveness instead of the way of retaliation towards those who have spoken untruths about me or who have attempted to damage my reputation by slander. Help me to express my anger with control towards my offenders and to realise that the way of revenge will only lead to more sadness. In your Spirit, may I find motivation, courage and peace in following your example, even though this might take some time. Guide me in choosing the right way to go about restoring my reputation.

I pray through Jesus Christ, Our Lord. Amen.

STANDING TALL

He entered Jericho and was going through the town when a man whose name was Zacchaeus made his appearance; he was one of the senior tax collectors and a wealthy man. He was anxious to see what kind of man Jesus was, but he was too short and could not see him for the crowd; so he ran ahead and climbed a sycamore tree to catch a glimpse of Jesus who was to pass that way. When Jesus reached the spot he looked up and spoke to him, 'Zacchaeus, come down. Hurry, because I must stay at your house today'. And he hurried down and welcomed him joyfully. They all complained when they saw what was happening. 'He has gone to stay at a sinner's house,' they said. But Zacchaeus stood his ground and said to the Lord, 'Look, sir, I am going to give half of my property to the poor, and if I have cheated anybody I will pay him back four times the amount'. And Jesus said to him, 'Today salvation has come to this house, because this man too is a son of Abraham; for the Son of Man has come to seek out and save what was lost'.

Luke 19:1-10

Identifying Obstacles

- Have I been critical? Unkind? Prejudiced towards another person? Envious? Jealous?

- Where is the envy in my life? Is there any trace of jealousy? Do they ever lead me into resentment and into being unfairly critical of anyone?

- What does Jesus' attitude say about how I relate to others, especially those of whom I am critical?

Reflection

A plant needs to be exposed to the sunlight in order to blossom and reach full maturity. In the light it stands tall, stretching out to its Creator. In the dark it shrinks, loses its colour and collapses in on itself. So it is with people who are, for example, downhearted, disappointed, lonely or marginalised. Their spirits are low and they feel small because of what has happened to them. By contrast, those who, for example, are given good news or have had something good happen to them may feel as if they are walking on air. In another way people who are criticised or frowned upon may find that their spirits are low and that they are made to feel small in some way. Positive and understanding comments lift people's spirits and make them feel tall.

Jesus had a lovely way of making people feel tall and lifting their spirits. He encouraged them and loved them to the extent that even those who had lived a wayward life began to follow him too. The story of Zacchaeus is a fine example of Jesus in his ministry raising the embattled spirits of others and making them feel tall. When Jesus saw Zacchaeus he said to him: 'Come down. Hurry because I must stay at your house today', and Zacchaeus 'hurried down and welcomed him joyfully'. His job as a tax collector had not made him popular with the people. He was despised in the community, which made him feel as small inside as he was physically. Without being asked by Jesus, he instantly made a promise: 'I am going to give half of my property to the poor and if I have cheated anybody I will pay him back four times the amount.' Obviously, there was kindness and generosity in Zacchaeus waiting to be expressed and perhaps he never found the opportunity to do this until his encounter with Jesus. He climbed up the tree a small man and came down a tall one – in this sense his spirit was raised by Jesus. No more climbing trees for Zacchaeus to see Jesus!

Jesus summoned all those gathered in the town that day to climb above their negative attitudes towards Zaccheaus and to celebrate the goodness in him and God's salvation for him. He also summons us to climb above our critical opinions of others. He calls us to rise above our jealousy and insensitive comments about people we know. Jesus always rose above the failings of others and raised their spirits, giving them a new sense of purpose and outlook in life. He may be calling us now to do the same for someone we know: a neighbour, a friend, a family member, a person in the community who would welcome a positive comment, or somebody in the workplace. In the story of Zacchaeus, God calls us to a new way of relating to people. We are valued by God, wanted by God and we are all equal in the eyes of God. God calls us to live the love that he offered Zacchaeus.

A PERSONAL RESPONSE

- Rejuvenate the spirits of people you know with words of compassion and encouragement.
- Ensure your criticism is always constructive.
- Give positive affirmations.
- Thank Jesus for rising above your failings.

A PRAYER FOR THE JOURNEY

Loving Lord,

Your healing words rejuvenated Zacchaeus and quickly prompted him into changing his lifestyle.
You do not condone the wrongdoings of people, but through your positive and affirmative words you help them discover the potential for goodness in themselves.
Give me, Lord, the gift of being more accepting of others and the insight to see their gifts. Help me to reveal in others their gifts by using constructive and compassionate comments.

I pray through Jesus Christ, Our Lord. Amen.

GENEROSITY OF TIME AND SPIRIT

> The Pharisees and their scribes complained to his disciples and said, 'Why do you eat and drink with tax collectors and sinners?' Jesus said to them in reply, 'It is not those who are well who need the doctor, but the sick. I have not come to call the virtuous, but sinners to repentance' ... The tax collectors and the sinners, meanwhile, were all seeking his company to hear what he had to say.
> *Luke 5:30-32, 15:1*

IDENTIFYING OBSTACLES

- How would I sum up the attitude of the tax collector? The Pharisee? How do I see these attitudes in myself?

- Do I judge?

- Am I self-centered?

- How important is appearance to me? Do I seek to appear better than others?

REFLECTION

The doorbell rang. When I opened the door I saw a dishevelled man standing humbly in the shadow of the doorway. I greeted him. 'Could you give me something to eat? I am a man of the road,' he said softly. 'Come in,' I replied. We shared some food and chatted for a while, even though conversation did not come easily to him – I thought this was possibly because he spent so much time on his own. I offered him some money and some food to take with him, but, strangely, he did not really want it. 'Thanks for the welcome,' he said leaving. Then he sadly said, 'Most people don't want to know me because I am a man of the road'. Later I realised that he was just very grateful to be welcomed and to rest a while, and that he was not calling for money. Loneliness appeared to be his constant companion.

There are many people in our communities who value people being generous with their time, such as the housebound, those who live alone and people in hospitals or in nursing homes. We all seek and value the company of others. Many of us need others to advise or to help us, to listen to us or just to be there for us – people value our time and our company.

Jesus welcomed everyone into his company. For him, nobody was better than anybody else. The 'tax collectors and the sinners were all seeking the company of Jesus to hear what he had to say'. It meant so much to them that there was someone who was very happy to talk and eat with them – they valued his friendship. Normally, these people were rejected by the rest of the community. Criticism and condemnation often flowed from the angry tongues of the Scribes and Pharisees as to why he kept such bad company. 'Why do you eat and drink with the tax collectors and sinners?' they queried.

Jesus excludes no one from his company. Others may abandon us, give up on us, alienate us or exclude us in some way, but Jesus always remains faithful to us even if we do not always remain faithful to him. Jesus takes a different attitude towards the sinners, the outcasts, the rejects of society, and those others do not want to be associated with. The Pharisees and the Scribes thought that because of their positions of importance they were above everyone else. Jesus reminded them that everyone is a child of God.

Leading by example, Jesus encourages us to change our attitudes towards others if we think we are more important than someone else because of our social standing or because we are more financially secure. We might not want to mix with others because they come from a particular place; we might not want to sit beside someone because we feel we are better than that person in some way; we might not invite a neighbour or a relative to a family celebration because they are less well-off than us. These are poor reasons for not welcoming others into our company. Jesus wants to change this type of attitude to others in us – he values the company of everyone. He invites us to value in a responsible way the company of people we meet daily and those we sincerely know would appreciate our presence.

A Personal Response

- Be conscious of the needy and those who feel excluded. Consider some practical ways in which you could help or support them.

- Go to see someone who would appreciate a visit from you.

- If you are feeling lonely or depressed, visit a friend who would re-energise and reinvigorate you.

- Spend some quality time in the company of Jesus, who always included others in his company.

A Prayer for the Journey

Loving Lord,

On the roads and the byways of life, you gave of yourself to all those who needed your time. You ate and prayed with the rejected, the undervalued, the broken-hearted, the lonely and the marginalised. You valued everyone who came to you and healed those who came for help.

Thank you, Lord, for the people who have been there for me and who have blessed me with their time. May I not be selective with my company to the exclusion of those who might need a friendly smile or a little support along the way.

I pray through Jesus Christ, Our Lord. Amen.

SPECIAL BRANCH

Scripture

> I am the vine, you are the branches. Whoever remains in me, with me him, bears fruit in plenty; for cut off from me you can do nothing. If you remain in me and my words in you, you may ask what you will and you shall get it. It is to the glory of my Father that you should bear much fruit, and then you will be my disciples.
>
> *John 15:5-8*

Identifying Obstacles

- How can I branch out to others more effectively?

- What tempts me to branch away from God?

- Do I branch out to values that are transient?

Reflection

During the summer months, the neighbours flocked to the small spring well with their empty, rattling buckets. They always left with the buckets overflowing with fresh, sweet-tasting, life-giving water. The small well, tucked in a corner of a rocky field, quietly and selflessly gave of itself because it was connected to a greater source, which entrusted to it the abundant gift of water. The neighbours always praised the source from which the small well sprang.

Similiarly, we come to God to draw life-giving water from him, which will nourish and refresh our life-journey to heaven. There is a beautiful connection between God and us. Jesus says: 'I am the vine, you are the branches.' In the same way that the branches get what they need from the vine, the vine also needs the branches. God's love for us is like the source that gives lasting water to the spring well. God calls us to be like the well for him, freely sharing the life and energy we have received.

Jesus says: 'Whoever remains in me, with me in them bears fruit in plenty, for cut off from me you can do nothing.' God cannot bring new life to others through us if we are 'cut off' from him. The challenge for us is to remain connected to God, the source of love. Electrical equipment is useless if it is not connected to a power supply. If we are not connected to God properly through prayer, the Eucharist, the Scriptures and acts of goodness, then God's work can never be done as effectively through us. Once we separate ourselves from the Lord we become like the 'withered branches' and God's work is left undone.

For us, staying connected to God, the source of love and goodness, involves pruning 'every branch in us that does not bear fruit'. The branches of the tree that produce good fruit are pruned seasonly; the old decaying branches, which impede the good branches from bearing more fruit, are skillfully cut off. Perhaps we hold on to dead branches that may hinder us from doing good work: old branches like addictions, self-interest, prejudices and gossiping, to name a few. While we hold on to these dead branches, the fruits of the Spirit (love, joy, peace, patience, kindness, goodness, gentleness, faithfulness and self-control) are impeded. During life's last moments, while we wait for God to call us from this life, worries about a poor pension plan in which we invested, or failing an important school examination or being overlooked for promotion in our job will not occupy our minds. Most of us will be more worried about concerns such as how we lived our lives, the love we gave to our families, how we reflected God's love to others, or how much time we spent in prayer.

God asks us to let go of the dead branches for the higher good to which he is calling us, so that those who come to draw life from God through us will leave refreshed and will praise God, the source of life.

A Personal Response

- Think of changes you need to make to fully restore your relationship with God. Reflect for a moment as to how you might go about making those changes.

- Make an effort to build happiness on values that will give you spiritual contentment.

- Think of a way in which you can offer more time to help a community-based activity.

A Prayer for the Journey

O Loving Lord,

You created me in your own image and likeness.
Your image in me is at its brightest when I remain in you.
There are times I want to do what pleases me.
You warn me of the dangers of idle pursuits.
Let me remain in you so that your love in me will branch
out into many good deeds.
Help me always to see beyond the things of this world and
to trust in the things of Heaven, which will never pass
away.

I pray through Christ, Our Lord. Amen.

BREAD FOR THE JOURNEY

> On this mountain, Yahweh will prepare for all peoples a banquet of rich food, a banquet of fine wines. On this mountain he will remove the mourning veil covering all peoples, and the shroud enwrapping all nations, he will destroy Death forever. The Lord will wipe away the tears from every cheek; he will take away his people's shame everywhere on earth, for Yahweh has said so. That day, it will be said: See, this is our God in whom we hoped for salvation; Yahweh is the one whom we hoped. We exult and we rejoice that he has saved us.
>
> *Isaiah 25:6-9*

IDENTIFYING OBSTACLES

- Do I attend the Eucharistic Table every Sunday?

- What are the obstacles that make me not want to go?

- Do I ever find myself inclined not to be there? Do I

rush to and from the Eucharistic Table? Do I think about what Jesus is really offering me at his table? Do I notice the others who are there? Do I show respect to them?

- Do I pray for God's healing love while I am there? Do I pray for others?

- What are my responsibilities to others when I leave?

REFLECTION

The table is a very important piece of furniture in a home. It is a place of meeting and eating, a place of nourishment and provision. The table is a place of conversation, sharing and encouragement. In many homes, the kitchen is like a sanctuary and the table is like an altar, occupying a special place. Many mothers (including my own loving mother) wore a cooking apron like a liturgical garment, where they prepared, prayed and presided over every meal. During meals, stories were shared about school life, and worries and joys were shared. Around the table, children were often comforted and corrected and family values nurtured. Prayers were taught. The table was a place of friendship and welcome where visitors and friends also gathered around.

Another table around which people gather is the table of the Eucharist, where we come together as the family of God to celebrate God's love for us and to be nourished by him. When Jesus ascended to heaven, he did not leave us on our own but promised to be always with us through the Holy Spirit, which we received at Baptism. By the power of the Holy Spirit, Jesus is present to us in the Eucharist. At the Eucharistic Table Jesus feeds us – the people of God – with his own body, which nourishes us on our journey to heaven. When we consume his body we nourish and deepen our connection with the Church, which is the Body of Christ. The loving relationship Jesus enjoys with the Father is offered to us. We are drawn together as one people. We listen to his Words in Scripture, which give us guidance and direction. We need the nourishment of the Eucharist to help us to grow more in the love of God and to live out his command, which is to love one another in the same way he loves us.

The table of the Eucharist connects us to the greatest table of all – the table in the kingdom of heaven. We are told that the Lord 'will prepare a banquet of rich food', where we will 'exalt' and 'rejoice' that the Lord 'has saved us!' We look forward to sitting at this table of 'rich food' with the entire family of God. While we are waiting to be called to the table in heaven we pray that, in the meantime, the Lord will continue to nourish us at the Eucharistic Table. We pray that we will listen to God's call to be the family that we represent in our gathering together. This will help us to prepare and be ready to be received at the table in God's Kingdom.

A Personal Response

- Honour Sunday as the most special day to attend the Lord's table. Thank Jesus for giving himself to you and for giving you a link to a wider community.

- At the Eucharistic Table, pray that Jesus can be nourishment to others through you.

- When you receive Holy Communion, ask Jesus to impart his strength to you to help you cope with your suffering. Connect Jesus' sufferings to yours.

A Prayer for the Journey

Loving Lord,

Thank you for inviting me and welcoming me to your table.

Thank you for giving yourself to me in the Eucharist to nourish me on my earthly journey to heaven.

Help me to grow more into your love each time I receive you. May my life then be a source of nourishment for others, helping them on their faith journey.

I pray through Jesus Christ, Our Lord. Amen.

REFLECTION IS DIRECTION

> Then he said to them, 'You must come away to some lonely place all by yourselves and rest for a while'; for there was so much coming and going that the apostles had no time even to eat. So they went off in a boat to a lonely place where they could be by themselves.
>
> *Mark 6:31-32*

IDENTIFYING OBSTACLES

- Do I have a hectic life with little or no time alone with myself or with God?

- Do I confuse material success with inner satisfaction?

- Do I rate myself on what I do rather than who I am?

- Do I allow my work and obligations to eradicate time for rest and recovery?

REFLECTION

Some people seem to run on the treadmill of life, moving with no direction, acting with no thought or working with no motivation, unable to get off. The promise of a visit to someone often gets postponed. Some people find it increasingly difficult to rise above the challenge to spend more quality time talking or listening to loved ones or friends. They may meet a friend or neighbour on a busy street and just manage a rushed 'Hello' or 'I'll visit you soon'. A year on, they may meet again only to be embarrassed into offering another promise to visit or phone.

If there is little time for oneself or for others, then there is probably less time or space for God. Due to the speed of the wheel of life, many promises to God evaporate in busy schedules: promises such as prayer, involvement in the community and visits to the church. People who go on retreats often say how great it is to be in a peaceful place, 'away from it all' – away from the business in their lives. For many of them 'away from it all' really means time to be in the presence of something else that is important to them: to connect anew with who matters most; to be on their own with God for a while with their thoughts or concerns; to say thanks to God for his goodness to them; or they may have a special intention they want to pray for. A quiet day away from it all is God's gift to us to spend sacred time with him. It gives us space and time to bow before our loving God without interruption and to reflect on what we are doing well for God.

Older people sometimes say, 'What is all this rushing about?' When one begins to get older, these wise words begin to make greater sense. Jesus in his time knew the importance of taking the apostles 'away to some lonely place' all by themselves to rest for a while. There was so much coming and going that the apostles did not even have time to eat. Jesus believed that his work for others was only truly possible when he spent sacred time with his Father in prayer.

Sometimes there is so much coming and going in our lives that there is little time to do something as simple as have a meal. We also need space and time away from it all to make sense of our lives and to discover new energies within us. God's work is carried out more effectively if we pause in prayer from time to time.

A Personal Response

- Slow down and make adjustments to your life that will give you a more fulfilling existence.

- Identify changes you could implement into your daily timetable that will give you more free time. Build some time into the pattern of your week, for God, yourself and others.

- Think of people with whom you need to spend more quality time. Imagine how both you and they might feel if you spend more time with them.

A Prayer for the Journey

Loving Lord,

Thank you for the gift of your time.
You are always there for me even though I do not always acknowledge it.
Make me more aware of the importance of spending quality time in your presence. Sometimes I become too caught up in the business and chaos of life that I do not give adequate time to you and to others. Through your Spirit, Lord, restore serenity and peace in me. Help me journey through the busy turbulent times to a more balanced and fulfilling existence.

I pray through Jesus Christ, Our Lord. Amen.

CORRECT LENS

SCRIPTURE

> You, my dear friends, must use your most holy faith
> as your foundation and build on that, praying in the
> Holy Spirit; keep yourselves within the love of God,
> and wait for the mercy of our Lord Jesus Christ to
> give you eternal life ... To God, the only God, who
> saves us through Jesus Christ our Lord, be the glory,
> majesty, authority and power, which he had before
> time began, now and forever. Amen.
>
> *Jude 20-21, 25*

IDENTIFYING OBSTACLES

- Do I integrate prayer into my life?

- Am I too busy to pray? When did I pray last?

- Do I pray only when I want something?

- Is prayer a means of manipulating God into giving me
  what I want?

- Do I persevere in prayer or do I give up too easily?

- Do I open myself to the presence of God's Holy Spirit?
  Do I leave time and room in myself for God's
  inspiration to reach through to me?

REFLECTION

For those who wear glasses, it is important that they are fitted with the correct lens for each eye. Without the correct lenses we are short-sighted or long-sighted, unable to see properly. While we may see enough to get by with, we are still blind to the finer details that enrich the picture of life.

Prayer may be compared to the correct lens, enabling us to see what we are missing, perhaps without knowing it. Prayer enables us to look within so as to reflect on the inner person, the spiritual side of our lives. We are well-advised to stand frequently on the sidelines of our lives to reflect on what we are doing well, what we can do better and what changes we need to make. If life is viewed only with short-sightedness that focuses on activity and achievement alone, we are forgetting something far more important. We do well to view life through the lens of prayer so that we might discover a deeper meaning to life. Prayer offers us the opportunity to reflect on the direction of our lives.

While in prayer, we become more aware of God's beautiful healing presence in us and in the world around us. Prayer offers us space to view our lives more through the eyes of God and less through the squinting eyes of the world. Prayer often provides the opportunity for us to reconnect with God and to disconnect from our old ways of seeing and doing things, and to begin afresh with a new vision of God and of life. Time given to prayer is God's gift to us to spend precious time with him. Prayer is our direct line, which is forever open to God. We may discover in prayer that God has plans for us too.

To help diminish the impact of the temptations of the world, Jude strongly encourages us to pray. He tells us to keep 'praying in the Holy Spirit', and to 'keep yourselves within the love of God, and wait for the mercy of our Lord Jesus Christ to give you eternal life'. Prayer provides us with a wonderful opportunity to connect our heart and minds with God and to help concentrate our energies to be more Christ-like in our actions, in our attitudes and in our outlook in life.

A Personal Response

- Look for prayers that say something to you. Remember everyone is different – what suits some people may not be helpful to you.

- Explore lives of people who have inspired you: family, neighbours, saints, the life of Jesus.

- Spend time in prayer each day and tune in to what God might be saying to you in your inner thoughts.

- When you are annoyed or anxious, open your heart to God in prayer to receive his healing presence. Persist in prayer even when you feel like giving up.

- Use your prayer to strengthen your relationship with God.

A Prayer for the Journey

Loving Lord,

Thank you for inviting me to spend time with you in prayer. Prayer is your gift to me to come and to take quiet time in your loving presence, regardless of what is going on in my life. Even when I cannot express in words what I want to say to you, you can still sense what I mean to say. Help me to leave with you all the negative aspects of what is happening in my life so that I can fully enter into your healing presence.

Strengthen my desire to pray always. Help me not to give up when I feel you are not listening or when I find it difficult to concentrate. Through your Spirit give me direction on my journey and strengthen my ability to stay focused on you.

I pray through Jesus Christ, Our Lord. Amen.

PLOUGHING A
HEAVENLY FURROW

SCRIPTURE

> As they travelled along they met a man on the road
> who said to him, 'I will follow you wherever you go'.
> Jesus answered, 'Foxes have holes and birds of the
> air have nests, but the son of man has nowhere to
> lay his head' ... Another said, 'I will follow you, sir,
> but let me go and say good-bye to my people at
> home'. Jesus said to him, 'Once the hand is laid on
> the plough, no one who looks back is fit for the
> kingdom of God'.
>
> *Luke 9:57-58, 61-62*

IDENTIFYING OBSTACLES

- Are my excuses for looking back persistently good
  enough?

- Do I complain to God and to others, always finding
  fault?

- Am I crowding my life with more people, things and
  activities that I can realistically engage with?

- Am I going off course? Am I losing my direction in life?
  What is the 'big picture' of my life?

REFLECTION

'Once the hand is laid on the plough, no one who looks back is fit for the kingdom of God' – anyone reared on a farm years ago would understand very well the meaning of this saying. Jesus' listeners also understood what he meant to convey in his words about the ploughman. Today the image of the plough might not be understood as well as it used to be because modern methods are different. The new sweat is that of machines' smoke steaming up into the air. Prior to modern machinery, fields were tamed and cultivated by more primitive devices and one of these was the horse plough. Documentaries about poverty in poorer countries frequently depict scenes of farmers tilling their land with a plough pulled by a horse or another animal.

Steering the plough pulled by a horse leaves its own wounds on the weary body of the farmer. If we examine these wounds or scars, we notice that they reflect those of Christ. Painful blisters emerge on the hands from gripping the plough tightly, which is important in the event of hitting a heavy stone. Otherwise, the plough might spring up and injure the farmer. To steer the scores in a straight line, the arms need to be outstretched at equal lengths. In the heat of the day, the salty sweat seeps into the dry, chapped lips. The handles of the plough sometimes pierced the farmers' sides when the plough struggled in the stubborn soil. During the days of poor footwear, sharp stones left severe marks on the soles of the feet. Nevertheless, the plough was gripped tightly to the last score until the ground was turned upside down.

The success of the ploughing was due to intense concentration on focusing ahead and not looking behind.

Jesus used the humble image of a plough to explain to us, his followers, what commitment really involves. He says to us that there can be no let-up in our promises and commitment to following him. Lack of time is a poor excuse to give for not doing his work. We either follow him or we do not; there is no middle ground and there is no looking back. Jesus calls us to grip tightly to the plough in persevering in our good works and in living out our commitment to him through our vocations. Gripping tightly to the plough of God's work brings responsibility and a new way of seeing things: being decent, honest, caring and respectful, being faithful in our commitments and being involved in doing God's work in the community. We are called to imitate the approach of the ploughman, concentrating fully on God's work and having a sense of God's vision within us.

Jesus gripped tightly to the plough of his mission, which was to save all people from sin and death. He never looked back. He succeeded in his Father's mission by incurring the wounds of the plough inflicted by our sins.

A Personal Response

- Reflect on the excuses you might give to Jesus for any lack of commitment.

- Explore the possibility of making new choices in order to follow Jesus more fervently.

- Reflect on the things that prompt you to look back negatively and that hold you back from following Jesus more whole-heartedly.

- Seek small ways that will help you to be more at the service of God.

- Ask God in prayer to renew and strengthen your resolve in your commitment to follow Jesus.

A Prayer for the Journey

Loving Lord,

Nothing deterred you from doing your Father's work, not even rejection, criticism or the cross.
Strengthen my resolve in following you without counting the cost, without reservation. Help me to remain faithful when I am tempted to 'look back' on the negative things of the past so much that I go off course in following you. May I make good choices that will lead to greater concentration to my commitment in doing your work.

I pray through Jesus Christ, Our Lord. Amen.

RENEWING YOUR PASSPORT

> Through towns and villages he went teaching, making his way to Jerusalem. Someone said to him, 'Sir, will there only be a few saved?' He said to them, 'Try your best to enter by the narrow door, because, I tell you, many will try to enter and will not succeed'.
>
> *Luke 13:22-24*

IDENTIFYING OBSTACLES

- What obstacle stands in the way of my journey towards heaven?

- Am I too easily diverted off my path to God?

REFLECTION

Some passengers appear anxious while waiting to go through the narrow doorway of the security checkpoint in an airport, for fear that they might be turned back. If they cause the alarm to trigger as they pass through, they are turned back and asked to try again. If their passports or documentation are not in order, they will also be turned back. The feeling of tension that envelopes the faces of some passengers as they approach the narrow doorway transforms into a smile of relief when they pass through it.

The image of the 'narrow door' can also be applied to other common life experiences. To achieve a goal or an ambition is like going through a 'narrow door' of discipline, commitment and sacrifice. People who achieve their ambitions in their fields of work may talk about the commitment, dedication and the pain that was required to succeed. To pass through the 'narrow door' of success requires much effort and in some cases many attempts. Perhaps, then, we should not be too surprised that Jesus describes the door into heaven as narrow and that it requires effort on our part to pass through it. He tells us to 'try your best to enter by the narrow door because many will try to enter and will be unable to'. God calls us to evaluate our lives, in other words, to reflect on what we are doing and how that is impacting on our journey to heaven.

Jesus' words to 'try your best' are very reassuring. These comforting words are, for example, said by parents to their children. We encourage others to try their best when giving them words of support. Many people try their best to struggle through each day, perhaps with depression, sickness or physical disabilities. Others do their best to get through the 'narrow door' of difficult experiences after many attempts, such as losing a loved one, losing one's good reputation or the end of a relationship. Though we may have made mistakes in the past, we try our best to get through them and move on, despite many failed attempts.

In a very encouraging way, Jesus is saying to us to try our best to enter by the narrow door into heaven. The door is open to everyone. Jesus invites us to go through it, but perhaps we turn ourselves away because we are unwilling to do what is required. We may fail at times or find it difficult, but the love of God is always there for us to help us get up again despite our many failed attempts on the journey to heaven. The door is open to all who wish to enter, but before we reach the door of heaven, it is important that our heavenly passports are in order.

A Personal Response

- Begin putting your documentation in order before you arrive at heaven's door:

  ✔ prayer life
  ✔ the Eucharist
  ✔ forgiveness
  ✔ good works
  ✔ letting go of selfish habits
  ✔ letting go of past hurts.

A Prayer for the Journey

Loving Lord,

Your heart was overflowing with love for people when you walked on this earth. Your encouraging words to 'try your best' helped many people to change their wayward ways and to follow you more closely.

Lord, inspire me each day to put my life in order and to try my best to imitate your example despite all my failings. Help me to grow in your love a little more every day.

I pray through Jesus Christ, Our Lord. Amen.